Reckless GRACE

Study Guide

Bill Vanderbush
Brit Eaton
Joe Bird

Acknowledgement

I'd like to give tremendous honor to my dear brother, Joe Bird, for seeing the vision for this study guide. Not only did Joe see the need for this companion piece, but with my permission, he took it upon himself to create it for our church life groups to use as a resource. It was so good at both simplifying and expanding upon the revelation of the book, I decided to make it available to everyone.

Joe is an example of a believer who is not merely a hearer of the Word, but he takes it and finds the means to apply it to create space to develop a Kingdom Culture in his world. To take what we claim to understand by intellect, and turn it into an experience that can be seen and shared is true Spiritual maturity. May we all find the grace of God so impactful. Thank you, Joe.

Bill Vanderbush

Part I – The Grace Message

"The joy that comes with being a steward of God's relentless, radical, reckless grace is simply too good not to share." – Bill Vanderbush

1. Grace Redefined

"If you forgive the sins of any, their sins have been forgiven them: if you retain the sins of any, they have been retained." John 20:23

Jesus was crucified, dead and buried. Three years of ministry ends brutally. Kingdom hopes of many are crushed. Shell-shocked disciples gather together in the upper room to pray, cry, and pray some more.   Jesus' death shouldn't have come as a surprise. He predicted it often enough, but they didn't understand. Maybe it was the brutality of His death. Maybe it was their secret hope that Jesus' Father in heaven would save Him, but no, now it's over. They huddle behind locked doors fearing for their own lives. Would the Jews murder them also?

Suddenly, Jesus is there….in their midst, saying "Peace to you." He's there with them! He's back! What thoughts must have been racing through their minds. Were they "Nothing can stop us now thoughts?" or were they, "Oh no, the Jews will try to kill Him again?" We don't know, but we do know this much; when Jesus showed up, everything changed!

In the midst of the shock and awe, Jesus does something totally unexpected. He breathes on them and says, "receive the Holy Spirit." God breathes on them! Only one other time in the history of mankind has God breathed on humans - when He first formed Adam from the dust of the ground and breathed the breath of life into him. By breathing on His disciples, Jesus, the last Adam, restored God's image and likeness back into his creation.

What Jesus says next is completely overwhelming: "If you forgive the sins of any, their sins have been forgiven them; if you retain the sins of any, they have been retained" – John 20:23 This passage is the scriptural linchpin for God's gift of grace to us. It can change your life and the lives of those around you who desperately need God's grace. But isn't God the only one who can forgive sins? How could we ordinary mortals be given this gift?

Before His death, Jesus had already given His disciples the power to perform miracles. Peter walked on water. Philip translated great distances instantly. Other apostles healed the sick, cast out demons and raised the dead. Everything Jesus did, a disciple also did, except for one thing – the forgiveness of sins.

Releasing forgiveness of sins through the love of God is the greatest supernatural gift Jesus imparts to us. After creation, we fall into sin. After the resurrection, we are restored to our original identity. Out of that identity comes power and authority in the spirit realm. The resurrected Jesus invites us to represent Him in everything, including His grace. You see, your sins (past, present, & future) were erased by Christ's atoning sacrifice on the cross. All we have to do is come into agreement with Him by surrendering our will by faith and receive His grace. This is what it means to align our heart and mind with His redemptive sacrifice.

We already have the gift of God's grace. We possess power and authority to forgive sins in Jesus' name. This may sound offensive to you. The gospel of Jesus Christ is offensive to our post-Christian culture. It comes down to accepting radical grace. Grace that makes no sense by earthly standards. Grace we cannot possibly steward faithfully in our own strength.

What is grace? Where did it come from? How do we get it? What does it cost? How will it change me? How do I control it? Can I control it? The questions go on and on.

Grace is not a thing. It's not a feeling. We can't create it, but we know where to find it. Grace is a person. <u>Jesus Christ is the embodiment of grace</u>. He is grace personified and He offers this encounter with His grace to all who believe. Jesus won't force you to accept it. Walking in His radical grace is a conscious decision we all get to make. It's a choice to be forgiven and in turn to forgive others. It's a choice to come into agreement with God about His opinion of you and everyone else created in His likeness.

Extending grace to others brings us into agreement with the redeeming love of a God who keeps no record of wrongs and asks us to love our enemies. Jesus offers freedom from the prison of sin. Jesus offers an outpouring of radical grace unlike anything you've ever received.

Jesus said that apart from Him we can do nothing and it's true.

We can't do anything in our own strength.

- •We can't forgive.
- •We can't heal.
- •We can't cast out demons.
- •We can't even hold onto our faith.

Receiving grace is uncomplicated, but there is a divine order to follow. Jesus speaks clearly in the Lord's prayer that to receive forgiveness, we must <u>first</u> forgive others. People may have made themselves your enemy, but you don't have to come into agreement with them. Nobody can be your enemy without your permission. Jesus wants us to love our enemies and do good to those who hate us. We also must forgive ourselves, which can be harder than forgiving others!

When you walk in your true identity in Christ, you won't be able to see people as enemies, but as broken beings who desperately need to encounter the God of grace.

The challenge of John 20:23 is this: Jesus is calling all believers to put on display the grace we believe God is providing, not just to the world, but to ourselves. We are invited to personally usher in the kingdom of God through His manifest grace, not because our salvation is dependent upon it, but because we're His children!

Reflections on grace defined:

  1. Do you struggle to extend or receive grace and forgiveness? Why or Why not?

  2. How would you explain grace to someone who is not familiar with it?

  3. What does John 20:23 mean for you right now?

  4. Which is harder to forgive: yourself or others? Why?

  5. How do you feel about forgiving someone else's sins?

2. Grace Received

"For it is in giving that we receive; it is in pardoning that we are pardoned; it is in dying that we are born to eternal life." – Saint Francis of Assisi

Until you have been filled with God's grace (and know it) you can't release grace to others. By learning to rest in the loving arms of our Father God, we embrace abundant grace for ourselves and share the overflow with others. Jesus released the gift of grace to his disciples (John 20:23) and He releases the same grace to us. When you're full of grace, sharing it with others becomes a natural outcome.

"For God so loved the world, That He gave His only begotten Son, that whoever believes in Him shall not perish, but have eternal life" (John 3: 16). These are powerful, oft-quoted words of scripture that point to God's intentions when He gave us the gift of grace through Jesus Christ. God gave everything to have us with Him for eternity. He didn't wait until we were good enough. While we were still lost in sin, He gave us His son, knowing full well that many would reject His precious gift.

"For God did not send the Son into the world to judge the world, but that the world might be saved through Him. He who believes in Him is not judged; he who does not believe has been judged already, because he has not believed in the name of the only begotten Son of God" (John 3:17-18). If you believe in Jesus, you are not judged. You are free! If you don't believe in Jesus, you judged, not by Jesus, but by your own unbelief. You are already guilty and dead in your sin.

Receiving God's grace is a fourfold agreement revealing what Jesus did:

1. For you (He forgave your sins)

2. To you (He restored you to innocence)

3. In you (He made you a home for His presence)

4. As you (He moves through you to release grace to others)

So, who condemns us? Who judges our actions as worthy or not? The Father isn't judging you (John 5:22). Jesus isn't judging you (John 12:47), so who is judging?

In John 12:48, Jesus gives us the answer. "He who rejects Me and does not receive my sayings, has one who judges him; the word I spoke is what will judge him at the last day." Why is the differentiation important? Because it allows you to see Jesus Christ for who He really is, and to see yourself for who you really are in Him.

God sent His Son to save us, not to judge us. Jesus came to invite you into a personal relationship with Himself, one that would change you forever. Jesus Christ came to restore the original identity you were given at creation so that you can choose obedience to the Word He speaks, not out of fear or obligation but as a joyful response to the grace He extends.

Jesus only says and does what His Father commands and the Father's commandment is our commission: to know the Father, the one true God, and Jesus Christ whom He sent. To "know the Father" is the definition of eternal life! So... it follows that eternal life has already been offered to us; we just have to say yes!

<u>Believe this good news and receive His reckless grace and be at peace</u>. You can't earn it, so please stop trying so hard. Just say yes! Let His goodness transform heart, mind, body and soul as you learn to release grace as Jesus did – in the overflow of grace received.

Not forgiving yourself is the most common barrier to receiving grace. Those feelings of worthlessness! Those mind games of convincing yourself that your sins are too great. Even when you make the intellectual case for forgiveness, somewhere deep inside, you don't believe you deserve it. God uses compassion to release healing and deliverance. Webster defines compassion as "sharing the painful feelings of others." It's putting yourself in their shoes and seeing/feeling what they see. Compassion ignites a shared feeling of mutual understanding that allows God's grace to displace pain.

Satan does not want you to forgive yourself. He wants you in bondage to sin. When you decide not to forgive yourself, you are choosing not to come into agreement with God. You are refusing God's grace. You may think it's humble to punish and withhold grace from yourself. Don't be deceived. It's actually coming from a secret place of pride. When God says, "You are forgiven," who are you to say otherwise? Your Father in heaven calls you His "beloved child." Nothing can separate you from His love (Romans 8:38-39).

Reflections on grace received:

1. Why is it so hard to forgive yourself?

2. Why do you feel forgiven on Sunday and guilty the rest of the week?

3. How does recognition of "Christ in you" help you understand and receive grace?

4. Do you believe <u>all</u> your sins are forgiven by God? Why or Why not?

5. Will you receive the gift of grace God has given you through the finished work of Jesus Christ?

3. Grace Released

"Lord, how often shall my brother sin against me and I forgive him? Up to seven times?" – Matthew 18:21

In the Old Testament, forgiveness was limited. Even the most God-honoring Jewish rabbis would suggest forgiving an offense "not more than three times" (Amos 1:3). Peter, wishing to impress Jesus in front of the apostles suggests forgiving an offense up to seven times. Jesus responds to Peter by introducing the concept of limitless grace! Jesus answered: "I tell you not seven times, but up to seventy times seven." (Matthew 18:22) This is a new concept for the apostles and the Jewish people. If Jesus sets no limits on forgiving brothers and sisters, how can we?

As the disciples eat breakfast with the resurrected Christ on the shore of the Sea of Galilee, Jesus demonstrates limitless grace for them. By standards of that day, Jesus would have every right to withhold forgiveness from Peter, yet not only does He forgive him, He restores Peter to his leadership position as head of his fledgling church. As disciples of Jesus Christ, we are commissioned and qualified to release that same reckless grace and forgiveness. The same grace that Jesus released to Peter is fully present within you now! Receive it in full, and release it, in Jesus' name.

Our human hearts are made to crave justice; we're wired to "get even" as part of our DNA. The problem with earthly justice is that it never delivers God's peace. The old covenant, eye-for-an-eye mentality doesn't satisfy the way we wish it would. Even when wrongdoers get exactly what they deserve for their crime, our hearts remain broken. A far better (although much harder) approach is forgiveness. Extending grace to a broken world, desperate for grace, brings

13

reconciliation and peace. God, in Christ, is reconciling us to Himself by not counting our trespasses against us. And now He has committed us to that same ministry of reconciliation. The sobering reality of God's gift of reckless grace is this: If the world doesn't know it's loved, forgiven, and filled with glory, it's not God's fault. It's ours.

Jesus gives us stewardship of His grace when He releases it over His disciples (in John 20:23). Be as radical or restrained as you want with this gift, but if you do what He calls and empowers you to do, you will set others free, just as Jesus did. **The tangible release of God's grace over humanity is quite possibly the greatest evangelistic tool that the church has never used**. Releasing that grace in the overflow becomes not only our right as a child of God, but your responsibility as a co-heir to the Kingdom of Heaven with Jesus Christ. This is the magnitude of the gift you carry!

You may be wrestling with the word *reckless* thinking, "God is not reckless so why use that word?" If Scripture has taught us anything, it's that grace brings about radical transformation in the hearts, minds, and lives of the most unlikely people. Reckless grace means being willing to position your heart toward forgiveness, no matter how great the offense. It means surrendering to the grace gift you have received and overflowing in it out of the sheer joy of possessing it. What it doesn't mean is giving a pass to someone who wrongs you. It doesn't mean enduring abuse or refusing to stand up for the powerless. Grace calls offenders out, "I do not condemn you, either. Go. From now on, sin no more". (John 8:11)

In the story of the Samaritan woman at Jacob's well (John 4), Jesus risks His reputation as a rabbi and a Jew by talking to a woman of Samaria. Jews had nothing but contempt for Samaritans and did not engage them. To speak with a

Samaritan woman is doubly offensive. Yet Jesus casts this custom aside by extending grace to this woman, speaking to her of "living water" (John 4:10) which is another way to describe grace. In her excitement, she runs to tell her village and as a result, many in her village believe in Jesus. For the opportunity to release grace and save souls, Jesus was willing to humiliate Himself before His apostles. A reckless act!

Reflections on grace released:

1. Why is God's grace offensive in our culture?

2. When it comes to grace, what does the word reckless mean to you?

3. The world sees God's grace as reckless. They may see you as reckless in releasing grace to others. How does that make you feel?

4. Are you willing to release grace even when the offender is not yet repentant, as Jesus did? Why or why not?

5. Releasing grace implies risk of rejection. How do you deal with that?

4. The Grace of God

"By grace you have been saved through faith; and that not of yourselves, it is the gift of God; not as a result of works, so that no one may boast." – Ephesians 2:8-9

We are all sinners, but if we focus on our past, we're in danger of staying there as "just a sinner saved by grace." If you are in Christ, you are a new creation – a child of God, a beloved son or daughter of the King. We were "just sinners," but no longer. We were once dead in our sin, but now we are alive in Christ. There is "no condemnation for those who are in Christ Jesus." (Romans 8:1)

The grace of God liberates you from the power of sin and death, so you can live free in the abundant life God calls you to enjoy. But it's not all about you. God wants to move in and through you to minister to others who need grace. God made you a "saint" set apart in a place of high honor. The authority He gives you comes with fantastic Kingdom responsibilities, including the forgiveness of sins through the release of God's reckless grace. But remember, releasing God's grace only works in the overflow of grace received.

When the woman caught in the act of adultery meets Jesus, she discovers she's not who she thought she was. Through grace and forgiveness, she is restored to her original identity and lovingly challenged to act accordingly. She moves from sinner to saint in a moment by the power of grace released and received. When Jesus says to her "Go and sin no more," He is empowering her to walk in her restored identity as a child of God.

There is a divine order here that we must initiate, recklessly and without fear about how it looks to others or how the individual might react. Jesus is calling us back to a place we were always meant to be, a place where we can freely release grace to those desperately in need. The divine order of grace is:

1. Believe that God initiates grace and gives it freely through the death and resurrection of Jesus Christ.

2. Receive grace as God's gift and call to forgive the sins of others.

3. Release grace from that place of overflow and forgive the sins of others by extending reckless grace.

4. Repeat over and over, releasing more grace as it flows from God to you, to those who need it.

The reckless grace of God demonstrates a love not born of this world. God's grace is love embodied in a person – Jesus Christ. God invites us to be part of the revelation of His love to the world through grace released in and through us. The hard part is this: You can't love beyond a revelation of how loved you are by God. You can only love because He loved us first. God gives you grace freely, but you can only keep what you're willing to give away. God's grace is contagious! Once you receive it, you can't help but give it away.

Reflections on the grace of God:

1. How has God's grace impacted your life?

2. How has God's grace impacted the lives of people you love?

3. Where would you go to find people who desperately need God's grace?

4. Would you be willing to extend grace to them? What might that look like?

5. What is holding you back from experiencing the fullness of God's grace? On the page below, write the biggest roadblocks you face in experiencing grace. If you don't know, pray this prayer. "Jesus, what is keeping me from experiencing Your grace?" Write what you hear.

Part II – The Cost of Grace

"Anything worth doing will cost you something."
– Bill Vanderbush

5. The Problem With Grace

"Harboring unforgiveness is like drinking poison and hoping your enemy will die." – Joyce Meyer

Unforgiveness is a human disease, one that keeps us broken and separated from God's grace. Unforgiveness poisons your soul, making you vulnerable to sin. Only by accepting grace and positioning your heart for forgiveness can you be healed of this rampant disease of the soul. Forgiving those who hurt you goes against everything your flesh demands in a human cry for justice. Only God can give you the power to forgive through reckless grace. You can't do it on your own strength. Trying harder gets you nowhere. Surrender is the key. You must let go and let God pour grace through you. The overflow of grace will pour from you to those you forgive. Remember, grace isn't a feeling; it's a person – Jesus. He wants to work in and through you to release grace and forgiveness to a world in great need of it.

Repentance is not a requirement for forgiveness. Many of us were raised with the false idea that to receive forgiveness merely meant we had to repent of our sins and "do penance" as a penalty for sin. Jesus clearly did not require the woman caught in the act of adultery or the thief on the cross beside Him to repent before He poured out grace and forgiveness to them. Scripture reveals to us that God initiates with grace and repentance is often (but not always) the result. He gives grace because that's who He is. The power of God's reckless grace on display in the moment of Christ's death likely impacted thousands of lives that day and in the days that followed. The important thing to take note of is Christ's commitment to initiation. He releases grace first so that offenders have an opportunity to be transformed and restored in response to His goodness and mercy. As ambassadors of Jesus Christ and His Kingdom, we are called to "go and do likewise".

Why is releasing grace so hard? We know we should extend grace, yet when the moment for it comes, we hesitate. Why? The allure of offense is thick in our culture and can be even thicker in our churches. Something inside of us wants to be offended. It makes us feel significant. Instead of initiating grace and finding the freedom we want, we often cling to unforgiveness and justify ourselves with self-righteous anger. In most cases our self-righteous anger is not a Godly anger (Jesus clearing the temple of thieves) but rather a prideful anger that is all about us.

"Everyone must be quick to hear, slow to speak and slow to anger; for the anger of man does not achieve the righteousness of God" (James 1: 19-20). As God's beloved children, we can experience more freedom in life today, by giving away the very thing that your flesh tells you not to. Grace. A radical, reckless grace that sets you free and blesses those who receive grace in your overflow. When you choose to accept God's invitation into radical grace, you may feel less than graceful in the release. You won't do it perfectly every time, so don't place unrealistic expectations on yourself. All you have to do is say yes and let Him do the work, in and through you.

God wants to bring healing and freedom into your life by meeting every core longing you could ever have – significance, safety, purpose, understanding, belonging, and love – with

Himself. God invites you into something better than your current condition. Releasing grace is all about coming into agreement with God about what He thinks of others. He invites us to turn away from unforgiveness and toward His goodness. In so doing, He reveals truth about our offenders. As we learn to see offenders from His mind's eye, we will understand when God says: "They're loved whether they know it, believe it, or choose to receive it." So how can we love our enemies? It starts with a simple choice. <u>Choose to honor your offender, in any way you can</u>.

Honoring people is choosing to see treasure in them by focusing on something good about them. Choosing to honor your offenders does not excuse their behavior, nor does it downplay what they've done, but it does soften your heart and break down barriers of offense. It can heal the disease of unforgiveness.

Reflections on the problems with grace:

1. Remember an example where you tried to forgive someone and found it difficult to do.

2. What was holding you back? How did you overcome that feeling?

3. Do you think it's fair to offer forgiveness first without waiting for an apology? Why?

4. If God will fill us with grace whenever we ask Him, why is it so hard to release grace?

5. Can you think of an example of "honoring your offender?" How did it help?

6. What one practical habit could you adopt now that would help you to release grace more often?

6. Count the Cost of Grace

"Those of you who do not give up everything you have cannot be my disciples." – Luke 14:33

Extending grace will cost you. You always have the choice to stay offended and nurse a grudge against whoever hurt you or your loved ones. Counting the cost of grace is a calculation of the consequences of something – a careless or foolish action taken against you. If you feel that the pain of extending grace might be worse than holding on to the offense, you're not alone.

Choosing to withhold grace and suffer from the disease of unforgiveness is a choice many take, but deep inside you probably know there is a better way. You know that healing lies on the other side of forgiveness and the price to get there may well be worth the pain.

You may find it useful to prepare a lament. A lament is a brutally honest petition to God where you name the offense, count the cost of forgiveness, grieve the consequences and find the strength to release grace to your offender in Christ's name. In doing so you'll find healing of your mind, body, heart, soul, and your will. Writing a lament allows you to process your pain with God in an honest manner. It may take time, but however long it takes, counting the cost of grace is worth your time. It will usher in freedom that you need to heal and draw you closer to Christ.

The first step is to clarify offense:

- Did "that person" sin against you?

- Did "that person" sin against someone you love?

•Did "that person" sin against God?

After clarifying the offense, it's time to clearly name it. Writing down the answers to these questions directly in your "Reckless Grace" book or personal journal is the best way to process your feelings honestly. You may need a friend to walk through this procedure with you. The steps that define offense are:

•Who offended you?

•What did he/she do?

•When did it happen?

•Where did it happen?

•Why did he/she do it?

•What was the impact on you?

•Do you own any part in it?

•What did it cost you?

•What will releasing grace cost you?

Now that you've named the offense and counted the costs associated with it, it's time to do the thing nobody wants to do; let it go and let God have it. It's painfully freeing. A great way to do this is to write another lament in the form of a prayer. The point is to open up to God with the offense that's keeping you in bondage so He can free you from it. You can write your lament directly in your book or your personal journal. It's critical to be honest about your pain with God. He already knows all about it.

The steps in a lamentation are:

1. Cry out to God – Call to Him by name and ask Him to draw near.

2. Share your complaint – Tell Him all about your anger, pain, heartache, or sadness.

3. Affirm your trust – Acknowledge you believe His promises are true.

4. Ask Him for help – Petition God and ask Him for discernment on what He wants.

5. Name your offender – Bring your offender before God. Let it all out no matter how raw.

6. Ask for His grace – Acknowledge that you can't extend grace without Him. Ask God to reveal any sin in your own life so you can receive and release His grace.

7. Praise Him anyway. – Even in your pain, even in your anger, praise God anyway.

8. Declare your assurance in His goodness. – Thank God in advance for what He's going to do through you and for you.

Reflections on counting the cost of grace:

1. What's the hardest thing about counting the cost of extending grace?

2. Why is important to clarify the details of offense?

3. Writing down your feelings impacts your mind far more than just thinking about the offense. Why does this matter?

4. Churches split over issues of unforgiveness and offense. How could this be avoided?

5.You may have never written a lament to God, yet it's basically a written prayer. Many of David's laments were turned into Psalms. Could you write one privately or publicly? Use the space below to record a prayer of lament to God. Practice vulnerability.

7. Pillars of Grace

"Truly, truly, I say to you, he who believes in Me, the works that I do, he will do also; and greater works than these he will do; because I go to the Father." – John 14:12

God's grace is meant for all of us. It is our role to release grace recklessly like our heavenly Father does, for our good and His Glory. Out of our identity as His beloved children, we live within the mystery of God's grace imparted to all. Three "pillars of grace" are necessary to believe in grace, receive grace, and release grace to your offenders:

Pillar 1: Passion

Throughout Scripture, Jesus demonstrated an unrivaled passion for grace and released it freely to bless His people. As a disciple of Jesus, we are called to embrace and embody His passion for grace through the Holy Spirit living in us, as a grace conduit. The word *conduit* originates from a Latin word that means "bring together." We receive grace from God and we channel that flow of grace to bring His people together. This gift of power comes with a responsibility to keep God's grace flowing.

Pillar 2: Process

Learning to live a life of grace and peace is a process; it's rarely a one-time event. The more you flow in God's grace, the more you'll see how the process can vary from person to person and situation to situation. Remember the steps of releasing grace from chapter 2:

    1. Believe it.

2. Receive it.

3. Release it.

4. Repeat.

God will guide you as you practice the process of releasing grace. As you follow His lead, you'll find a greater revelation of His grace in your life. Others will notice and you will find that it leads you to a place of healing and victory where you're always ready to usher in the gift of grace for others through prayer, declaration, and anointing.

Pillar 3: Prayers

Prayer is the most powerful gift you can give or receive. On days when the grace you've been given feels out of reach, walk through the written prayers in Reckless Grace and find healing for your soul, energy for your ministry and a fresh revelation of grace from God. If possible, speak these prayers out loud, for your voice carries healing power for your soul.

Prayers for Grace:

- Revelation of love from the Father

- Strength in the struggle with offense

- Struggles with misdirected anger

- Grace for a difficult discussion

- Learning to forgive yourself

- Learning to forgive others

- Restoration and reconciliation in damaged relationships

Declarations:

- Declaring grace

- Declaring forgiveness

- Declaration of grace anointing

- Declaration of grace commissioning

The Holy Spirit empowers us to be one with God. You have been invited to an encounter with the Good Shepherd and to be led by His voice. As you hear God's voice throughout the day, make yourself available and flexible enough to be molded and shaped by God.

Scripture Proof Points – Memorize and they will serve you well as you release grace.

> Jesus gave you the power and responsibility to forgive sins. (John 20:23)

> God always initiates with grace (Mark 2; John 8; John 4)

> Forgive and you'll be forgiven. Don't and you won't. (Matthew 6:14)

> We are ministers of reconciliation by the power of God's grace. (2 Corinthians 5:18)

> You already have every virtue needed to steward God's grace (2 Peter 1:3-9)

Reflections on pillars of grace:

1. Jesus is offering us a life of grace received and grace released. Which one of the three pillars of grace – Passion, Process, & Prayers needs your attention now and why?

2. Try reading the grace prayers and declarations out loud. How did it feel? Was there power in the spoken word?

3. Jesus was adamant that His followers could and should do the works He did and more. How would that reality change your life? Use the space below to record a prayer request to God. Where do you need breakthrough.

Part III – Grace and Glory

"A revelation of authentic grace brings about a physical manifestation of joy." – Bill Vanderbush

8. Grace in Action

"When Moses was coming down from Mount Sinai (and the two tablets of the testimony were in Moses' hand as he was coming down from the mountain), Moses did not know that the skin of his face shone because of his speaking with Him." – Exodus 34:29

When you spend time with God, it shows. The presence of God affects what you do, how you do it and how you look. When Moses came down from Mount Sinai after 40 days with God, his face reflected God's glory. His appearance was so remarkable that it frightened the Israelites, forcing Moses to wear a veil so people could still be near him.

The glow of glory that Moses carried was attached to the old covenant between God and the people of Israel – something that was beginning to fade away to make way for something much better. God was preparing a new covenant with His people, one forged in the blood of Jesus Christ. The apostle Paul laid out stark contrasts between the two covenants:

1. The old covenant was written on tablets of stone; the new covenant is written on our hearts.

2. The old covenant was the letter of the law; the new covenant is of the spirit.

3. The old covenant brought condemnation; the new covenant brings righteousness.

4. The old covenant had a glory that faded; the new covenant has a glory beyond compare, one that will never fade away.

The old covenant was never made to last. Moses' glory glow was always meant to fade. As disciples of the new covenant, we are meant to wear God's unfading glory differently, unapologetically unveiled. It's from a place of unashamed boldness that we are able to put the glory of God on display to the world through manifest grace. The glory of God is synonymous with the goodness of God. God is longing to show the goodness of His glory to the world, and He wants you to show them through the reckless grace He gives you to release to others.

But what happens when the inevitability of trouble shows up in your life? When all those little problems disrupt your day? When some guy cuts you off in traffic, when your children disobey you, or when someone you trust betrays you? Let's face it, sometimes it's hard to get through a single hour without offense. The emotions that you feel from these offenses are real and worthy of acknowledgment. They can even be helpful as you name your offenses and dismiss them by way of grace.

When our identity rests in anything other than sonship in Jesus Christ, we are tempted to see offenses as personal injustices rather than opportunities to extend grace. The enemy uses our human condition to drag us back into our old man identity of sin, the one that has yet to receive God's grace and cannot yet release it. Take heart! God will teach you His ways of grace if you let Him, and His grace is there for you in the meantime.

Cling to grace in every moment! Consider the bigger picture of each situation. Maybe the guy who cut you off in traffic is late to an interview for a job he desperately needs! Maybe your children are just trying to get your attention because they want to be with their Dad. Maybe the person who betrayed you is crippled with regret? Can you extend grace to these people for their offenses against you, even in part? Can you find some small thing to honor in them? When you extend grace in the moment, it snowballs. When you forgive, it affirms the grace of God flowing in your veins and it makes you increasingly aware of the glory of God surrounding your grace interactions. A drop of grace is all it takes to start an outpouring that fills to overflowing in your life and in theirs.

You may wish to go back to the lament you wrote from chapter 7 and reflect upon it. Be honest with yourself. Are you ready to move deeper into the reckless grace you've been given by giving grace away? Some points to consider as you go deeper into releasing grace:

• Thank God for his grace – look for ways He has forgiven you.

• Ask God to take the burden of offense from you – affirm His way is better than yours.

• Surrender your fear, pride, rage, and pain. He can have it all.

• Ask Him to fill you up with His grace.

• Ask Him to reveal how to release grace.

Reflections on grace in action:

1. We all have "hot buttons." When they are pushed, we react quickly and negatively. How could releasing grace interrupt this cycle and make you a better person?

2. Can you think of an example where you chose to honor a person rather than react negatively to their offense?

3. Can you tell when people you know spend time with God? What changes do you see?

4. Many people find themselves stuck between the old covenant of law and the new covenant of spirit. How can releasing grace help them embrace the new covenant?

9. Opportunities for Grace

"Bless the Lord, O my soul and forget none of His benefits; who pardons all your iniquities, who heals all your diseases; who redeems your life from the pit, who crowns you with lovingkindness and compassion." – Psalm 103:2-4

As Son of Man, Jesus did nothing in His own strength. Although fully God, He humbles and empties Himself of any supernatural ability. He lives just as you and I do – in sheer obedience to the Father and to the leading of the Spirit. He is still fully God, not a created being, but He is also fully man – demonstrating the most "normal" Christian life in history. Every time Jesus refers to Himself as *Son of Man*, He's showing us what is possible for every person freed from sin and surrendered to the power of the Holy Spirit. *You have the same right and power on earth that Jesus did.* To heal the sick. Raise the dead. Cleanse the lepers. Drive out demons. And yes, to forgive sins. Imagine the sheer magnitude of the gift you carry!

As we see from Luke's account of healing the paralytic man, Jesus Christ has the power to forgive and heal in a single breath. As a believer who has received the gift of grace released by Christ (John 20:23), you have this same power flowing through your veins by your new birthright in Christ Jesus. Now don't be confused. It's God who forgives in and through you. It's God who heals, in and through you. And if we take on the mind of the Son of Man, doing what God does, saying what He says, we will witness the fullness of the grace and glory of the living God here and now. Everything Christ did, he empowered you and I to do, including giving grace away.

Grace is the mark of leadership in God's Kingdom. Division and denominationalism are human inventions, spawning from offense. We are all one body and one spirit. And in that spirit of unity, we are called to grace, peace, and love in each and every interaction we face. Grace is key in fostering authentic community in the body of Christ. As believers we are on the cusp of a grace revolution that will rival any revival we've seen to date.

Consider the places that could use a fresh revelation of God's grace. How might grace transform:

- Your family

- Your marriage

- Your church

- Your parenting

- Your ministry

- Your political party

- Your neighborhood, your country, and your world?

Reflections on opportunities for grace:

1. In what area might extending grace have the greatest impact in your life?

2. How will extending grace impact your leadership/hero-making?

3. What words will you use to inspire people around you to consider grace over offense?

4. What do you need to "un-learn" about grace?

10. The Embrace of Grace

"God was in Christ hugging the world to himself" – 2 Corinthians 5:19

Bible translations often have words in italics. This is not for emphasis, but rather to indicate that these italicized words were not in the original manuscripts, but were added by the translators for style, flow, or deeper cultural understanding. This is a common practice that generally aids in our understanding of scripture.

The primary Bible verse for Reckless Grace is John 20:23 – "If you forgive the <u>sins</u> of any, *their <u>sins</u>* have been forgiven them; if you retain the <u>*sins*</u> of any, they have been retained." (New American Standard Bible- NASB) The word "sins" appears three times in the NASB translation of this verse. They are underlined for easy reference. Two instances of the word "sins" are in italics and one occurrence isn't. Let's take a closer look:

• The first "sins" isn't italicized, so it existed in the original manuscript.

• The second instance – "their sins" is italicized so these two words were not in the original manuscript. Removing these words does not change the meaning of the verse.

• The third instance of the word "sins" is italicized and when you remove the word, the meaning of the verse changes.

The third "sins" in italics matters greatly because without it, we have a huge question. What, or perhaps, who is being retained? Jesus isn't talking about retaining sins at all in this third reference. He's talking about people. "The community that forgives sins must hold fast those whom it has brought into the community of eternal life" (Sandra M Schneiders, I.H.M- Jesuit School of Theology, Berkeley, California).

The word "retain" means to hold, seize, or keep possession of. Jesus doesn't want us focused on the holding onto or letting go of sin. He wants us focused on the holding onto or letting go of the person. When we choose forgiveness, we separate the individuals from their sin. We learn what it means to hate the sin and love the sinner, as Jesus did. When you see your offenders apart from their sin, it changes everything.

The first half of John 20:23 is enough and it's the expectation: if we forgive sins, they're forgiven. The second half is the real challenge: If we retain them, they're retained. It's not intended to be negative reinforcement of the grace gift, because it's not about sin. It's about people. It quite simply means *if you embrace them, they're held*. You have a choice to make. Will you hold them in contempt? Or will you hold them in the embrace of grace as the Spirit leads you?

In Scripture, sinners are drawn to Jesus because he is willing to embrace people separate from their sin. The people who followed Jesus didn't understand the fullness of His grace, they just wanted to be near Him. They simply chose to say yes to Jesus and His grace. Jesus doesn't hold on to sin or hold back His forgiveness. He holds onto people.

But what about boundaries?

How do we release God's grace without enabling sin or even putting ourselves in jeopardy? The answer lies in the embrace of grace, a force that supernaturally transcends space and time. How do you release grace to someone who betrayed you, abused you, or manipulated you? You know some people aren't safe, but you believe God wants you to release grace to them. As a grace-filled believer, you need to create sensible boundaries in order to guard your heart and life for kingdom purposes. Look to Jesus for examples. Christ gave Himself for everyone but did not entrust Himself to everyone. Grace does not require you to give yourself to anyone, especially those who have harmed you and may cause more harm. But grace does require that you love them, even when you can't possibly love them in your own strength.

Follow Jesus' example:

Jesus prioritized His time, energy, and affections for people who wanted to be with Him most. He had a group of about seventy regular followers, twelve disciples, and an inner circle of three: Peter, James, and John. This resulted in rivalries but allowed Jesus to make the deep investment the apostles needed to become disciples who knew how to make disciples – by being for all and to a precious few. Most importantly, Jesus regularly slipped away to be alone with the Father which was His highest priority.

Love-based priorities:

1.Love God with all your heart, all your soul, all your mind, and all your strength. Yes, all yourself. When God is first on your list, love is no longer a finite resource, it's infinitely renewable. You can give Him everything and He refills you with even more love and grace than you had in the first place – so much, you can't hold it all in; you have to give it away.

2.Love your people of peace. These are the precious few you give yourself to; the relationships you invest significant time and energy into. It could be your spouse, a dear friend, someone you disciple or someone who disciples you.

3.Love everyone else. These people are your "neighbors" as Jesus described in the parable of the Good Samaritan. Although you are not called to give yourself to them, you are called to give your life for them, as Jesus did.

A final word of caution for the embrace of grace: check your heart motives. Are you driven by sympathy or compassion? Sympathy is powerless – it's all heart, no solutions. When we move out of sympathy, we move in our own strength, full of fear and brokenness. Compassion is an empowering force. God moved Jesus with compassion before He performed His greatest miracles. When we move out of compassion, we move as one with God, full of power, love, and grace. Start small.

Focus on the person right in front of you. Be open to the leading of the Holy Spirit as you discern who to give yourself to and for. Stay flexible to be moved with compassion when God calls you to rise up and release His grace.

You already have the gift of grace. It's been yours since before you were born. The time has come for all followers of Christ to believe it, receive it, release it, and repeat over and over. You will never be ready in your flesh, only by God's spirit within you. Make grace a conscious choice of surrender, not a feelings-based reaction. You won't do grace perfectly, and that's okay. The goal is not perfection, but refinement.

You are now an ambassador of grace and as you share this incredible gift, you will see grace abound in your own life. We will all become grace apostles, instrumental in raising up a generation of grace-filled believers poised to bring God's kingdom on earth in all its fullness. The joy that comes with being a steward of God's relentless, radical, reckless grace is simply too good not to share. So, go and be blessed!

Reflections on the embrace of grace:

1. Think about the people in your inner circle. What do they have in common?

2. What would it take to add a few more "people of peace" to your circle?

3. Why is it good to have a Paul (mentor) and a Timothy (disciple) in your circle?

4. Why is compassion so much more powerful than sympathy?

5. What is the distinction between giving yourself for someone but not to them?

The 11th Chapter

The Baptism of Innocence
(Based upon a conversation between Bill Vanderbush and Charlie Coker)

Whenever I preach this message, the word *innocence* always comes to my heart. It's the most accessible understanding of the term *"justified."* It's one thing to believe we are forgiven. It's another to believe that we are innocent.

My dear friend and brother in the Spirit, Charlie Coker, who I wrote about in Reckless Grace, began to get a revelation of innocence as his marriage, children, and life were recovered and restored. The following paragraphs are taken from a conversation processing the revelation of innocence.

Losing Your Religion, and Restoring Your Innocence.

When we get into a performance-based religious system of discipline, we lose our innocence. Innocence is a weapon against immaturity and can restore childlikeness without religion. It's the baptism of innocence that restores our childlikeness. Without the innocence of a child, you won't let the Father tell you who you are.

Grace is not a means to excuse immaturity. Grace is an offensive empowerment for us to walk in holiness, not a defensive excuse to walk in sin. Innocence makes us a student and a son, and that redemption becomes our character. Innocence is what softens the hardened heart to bring tears to the preaching of the Gospel again.

Jesus didn't just forgive your sin. He became your sin. He's not afraid of sin. If He was afraid of sin, he would have never gone looking for Adam and Even when they fell. His righteous annihilates sin. Innocence is the death of distance from a holy God. Innocence is the greater dimension of the Kingdom, beyond even forgiveness.

Charlie shared the story of a woman whose husband was unfaithful to her and even though she forgave him, she didn't trust him. God began to deal with her and one morning she woke up, rolled over, and declared him innocent. When he awoke, he got up a new man and she had a new marriage.

Kings shift and move kingdoms by decree and declaration. We are kings on the earth and priests unto God, so our words carry power. A declaration of innocence restores the standard in the Spirit, shifting the atmosphere so one who was formerly guilty can be vulnerable before a holy God without fear. When Jesus was on the cross, he put the Father's heart on display saying, "Father, forgive them, for they know not what they do." He wasn't appealing to a reluctant Father to forgive a humanity enslaved to sin. He said that He only said what the Father was saying. So on the cross, He was putting the Father's heart on display.

To us, forgiveness and innocence are different, for we take pride in our record of wrongs. But our Father, who casts our sin as far as the east is from the west, takes forgiving us so deep that in His eyes we are innocent. Without that innocence, there is no true intimacy.

The baptism of innocence is an invitation to intimacy. Intimacy is the enemy of religion. The religious spirit operates through fear, intimidation, guilt, and shame. Intimacy requires that we let go of all of that. A baptism of innocence is the waterfall of grace that washes us clean from the stains of shame.

Without a revelation of innocence we approach God from a place of performance and not intimacy.

Innocence will mature you beyond your previous behavior. Innocence positions you to receive discipline properly. When the Father disciplines you, He is dealing with a root of false identity. The only proof of sonship is discipline. With innocence, the discipline isn't punishment for sin. It's the invitation to surrender into maturity.

Can you consider your enemies innocent? Can you face your offender and declare them innocent? The baptism of innocence is the only way we can bless our enemies.

Innocence doesn't declare that what a person did was okay. Your pain is valid. Your offender was wrong. No amount of revenge or vengeance or violence will take the pain away. Only Jesus can do that. When we give grace away, we are baptized in innocence. Innocence destroys the record of wrong. Love keeps no record: No record of wrong, no record of offense, not even a record of what you've been forgiven for.

Guard your memories and take them captive to the revelation of Christ. If you dwell on the memories of your past, your creative power has the ability to recreate the feelings, the guilt, and the shame that should no longer exist if that past has been erased by Divine blood. Our goal is to imitate Christ. How can an unholy human imitate a holy God incarnate without being phony? The old man and sin nature is the lie. Your reconciled union with Christ is the true reality.

Letting go of the idea that you have a sin nature is hard, especially if you've developed a habitual lifestyle that has chained you to an addiction. You may think that it's all Adam and Eve's doing that implanted this "thing" within you. But look at Genesis 4:7. God comes to Cain and says, "...sin is crouching at your door. It's desire is for you, but you must master it." What God doesn't say is that sin is within you because of what your parents did. A sin nature is a choice, and even the desire to make a choice doesn't prove that you have a sin nature.

Adam and Even had no sin nature, for they were made in the image and likeness of God and He declared they were very good. Yet believing a lie, they still had the ability to choose to sin. Your ability to choose to sin is no validation that you have a sin nature. Romans 6:6 says that our old self was crucified with Christ so we would no longer be slaves of sin. Sin is a lying slavemaster and pounds on our door for attention.

In Revelation 3:20, there is another said to be knocking at the door of our lives. Jesus says, "Behold I stand at the door and knock. If anyone hear my voice and open the door, I will come in and we will break bread together." He's not coming in with the first order of business being to tell you what you're doing wrong, or to even fix everything that's broken. His first priority is to share life and build relationship. Other things will be dealt with in time, with you and Christ working together. He's a good Father, the finest teacher, and the most engaging storyteller. And, oh, how He loves.

If we could see, just a glimpse behind the veil, into the unseen realm, perhaps we would never cease worshipping. The hymn writer found a revelation one day and penned one of my favorite lyrics. Perhaps there has never been a better use of the English language than to construct this song.

46

There is a fountain filled with blood
Drawn from Immanuel's veins
And sinner plunged beneath that flood
Lose all their guilty stains

They dying their rejoiced to see
That fountain in his day
And there may I, though vile as he
Wash all my sins away

Twas there, by faith, I saw the stream
Thy flowing wounds supply
Redeeming love has been my theme
And shall be till I die

I sometimes wonder, on the day Jesus was crucified, if a young man with dusty feet and scars on his soul stepped forward through the crowd. Perhaps slowly, yet with heaving lungs of desperation, he navigated the rocky terrain, walking toward the trio of crosses before him. With soldiers watching, he comes to the center cross, stepping beneath the shower of dripping blood to embrace the soaking wood. Having seen what this man could do, having witnessed him raise the dead, having seen him silently absorb religious judgment, having seen him beaten beyond human recognition, and having witnessed the compassion in His eyes through it all, to be drawn to come to stand beneath this cascade of crimson. Would you have been him? Would you have taken that chance? Today, with this book before your eyes, Christ bids you come.

To see who you really are, receive His baptism of innocence. Embrace the cross, and let the blood of the innocent Savior wash over you. Be clean and be free in the Name of Jesus Christ. For beyond the cross is the resurrection that validates our innocence, once and for all.

For more about the baptism of innocence, visit the website of Pastor Charlie Coker, Identity Church, Deltona, Florida. www.getgod.org

Grace and Peace to you.

"You are in Christ."
1 Corinthians 1:30

About Bill

Bill Vanderbush is a third-generation minister who has pastored for over twenty-five years. He and his wife, Traci, had a supernatural encounter with the Holy Spirit that drew them into an incredible adventure of being shaped and fashioned by the power and grace of God.

Bill's consuming passion is to empower people to do the greater works that Jesus spoke of and live out the mystery of our union with Christ. Bill and Traci's ministry invites people into a spontaneous, Holy Spirit-led, team ministry training experience that will forever transform the way you see and do life. Through this message and revelation of the grace of God, you will be liberated and empowered to invade the impossible.

Bill and Traci currently live in Celebration, Florida. They have two grown children, Britain and Sara.

Contact Bill

Facebook: www.facebook.com/billvanderbushpublic

Website: www.billvanderbush.com

                www.vanderbushministries.com

Instagram: www.instagram.com/billosopher59

Twitter: www.twitter.com/BillVanderbush

About Brit

Brit Eaton is a writer, speaker, discipler, and all-around pursuer of the kingdom of God. She helps corporate, nonprofit, and ministry leaders find the words to say to move people to action. An eager apostle and strong advocate for women in ministry, Brit thrives in diverse, Spirit-filled environments committed to unity in the body of Christ.

Brit lives with her husband, Mike, and daughter, Bella, in Mount Vernon, Ohio.

Contact Brit

Facebook: facebook.com/briteaton

Website: www.briteaton.com

Project 24

Project 24 is sold at live events as a USB flash drive and contains more than twenty-four hours of teaching that will impact your perspective of your identity in Christ from a wide variety of angles. Upon purchase, you will be sent a link to a web page where you can stream or download all twenty-four hours of the audio and video files.

Messages Include:
- Stewarding the Grace of God
- Out of the Wilderness
- You Are the Glory That Covers the Earth
- Understanding the Mysteries of God
- Being Love in the Darkness
- Walking in Identity and Authority
- Living Free from Sin Consciousness
- The Vengeance of God
- What Does God Believe about You?
- Empowering Women in Ministry

and many more.

Buy at: billvanderbush.com

Presence and Power

Presence and Power is sold at live events as a USB flash drive and contains more than twelve hours of teaching on walking in the supernatural life that Jesus Christ has given to you. This download also includes PDF files of notes for some of the messages. Upon purchase, you will be sent a link to a web page, where you can stream or download all twelve hours of the audio and PDF files.

Messages Include:

- Spiritual Joyfare
- Overcoming Demonic Influence
- Living in the Presence
- Being a Student of the Spirit
- Greater Works Will You Do
- Increasing in Favor
- Words of Knowledge
- Healing and Miracles

and many more.

Buy at: billvanderbush.com

Vignette: Glimpses of Mysterious Love

by Traci A. Vanderbush (Author),
William H. Vanderbush (Contributor)

Raw, unstructured, free-flowing. Love is an indefinable mystery. This is one couple's attempt, after learning the art of falling in love with each other once again, to articulate the limitless depths of the human soul. Through various journal entries, thoughts, and poetic expressions regarding love, mercy, grace, and sexuality; join them on this journey of glimpses into mysterious love.

Buy at: www.billvanderbush.com

Made in the USA
Columbia, SC
26 July 2019